# HOCKEY

BY KARA L. LAUGHLIN

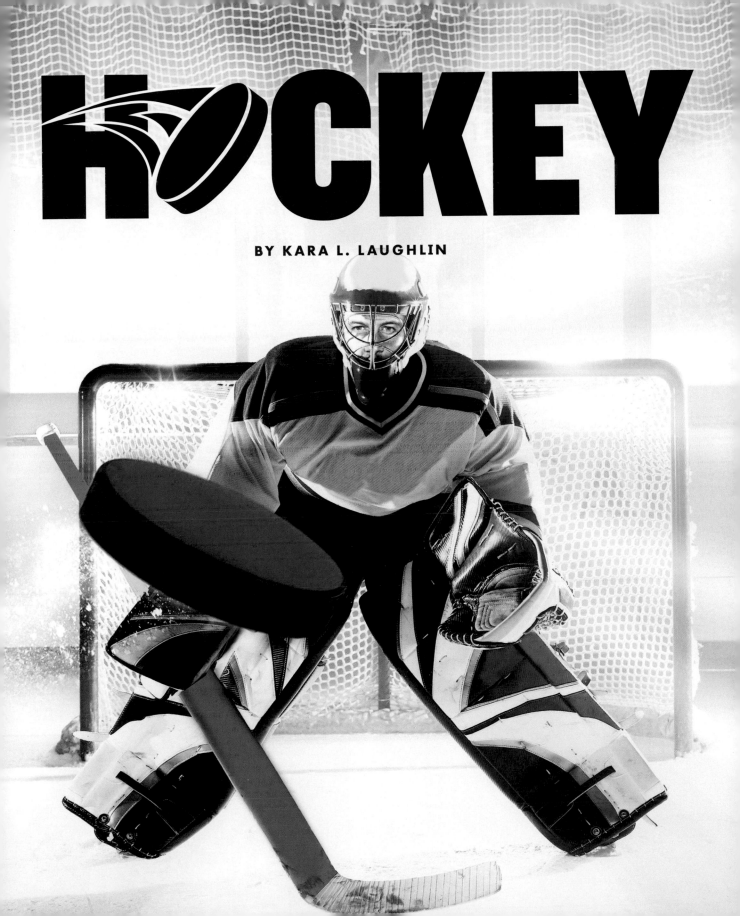

The
Child's
World®
childsworld.com

Published by The Child's World®
1980 Lookout Drive • Mankato, MN 56003-1705
800-599-READ • www.childsworld.com

ACKNOWLEDGMENTS
The Child's World®: Mary Swensen, Publishing Director
The Design Lab: Design
Heidi Hogg: Editing
Sarah M. Miller: Editing

PHOTO CREDITS
© Ahmad Rashdan/Shutterstock.com: 15; enterlinedesign/
Shutterstock.com: 9; gilaxia/iStockphoto.com: 13; Joe Christensen
/iStockphoto.com: 20-21; John_R_Baldwin/iStockphoto.com:
16; Kenneth C. Zirkel/iStockphoto.com: 7; Lorraine Swanson/
Shutterstock.com: 10; Michael Braun/iStockphoto.com: 19;
photographer2222/Shutterstock.com: cover, 1; Rob Fox/
iStockphoto.com: 4; Vaclav Volrab/Shutterstock.com: 2-3

ISBN: 9781503807778
LCCN: 2015958123

Printed in the United States of America
Mankato, MN
June, 2016
PA02300

# TABLE OF CONTENTS

4

# Let's Play Hockey!

Get a **puck.** Grab your stick. Lace up your skates. It is time for ice hockey!

# Equipment

To play ice hockey, you need skates and a puck. A helmet protects your head. **Pads** take care of your body. Padded gloves are important, too.

Lastly, you need a hockey stick. You use the stick to hit the puck.

**Fast Fact!**
Hockey sticks are different heights.
The curved end of a stick is called the blade.

# The Rink

A hockey rink has a red line in the center. It divides the rink in half. There are two blue lines. They break the rink into **zones**.

There are also nine **face-off spots**. Five of the spots have circles around them.

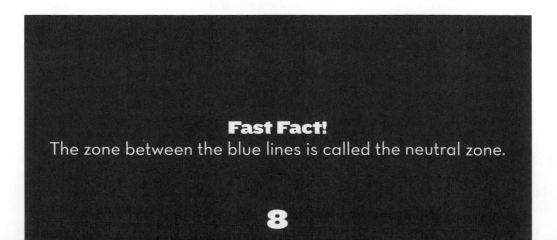

**Fast Fact!**
The zone between the blue lines is called the neutral zone.

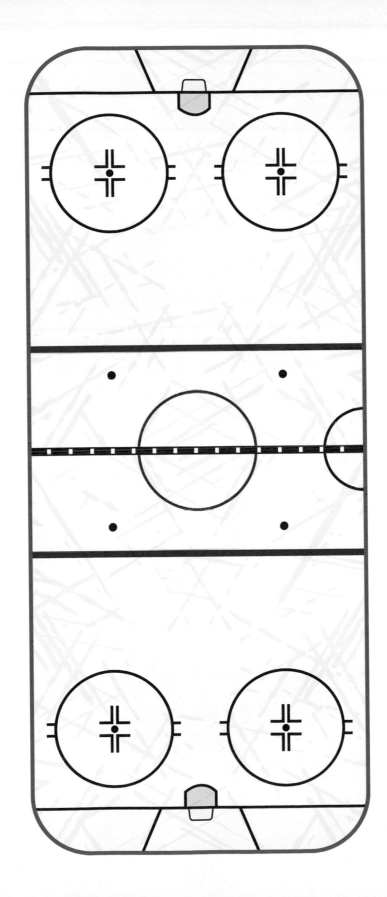

# Players

There are six players on each team. Some focus on scoring. Some defend the net.

The **goalie** stays near the net. She blocks the puck to keep the other team from scoring.

**Fast Fact!**
Goalies wear more pads than other players. They have larger sticks and special gloves, too.

# Face-Off!

The game begins in the center **face-off circle**. One player from each team enters the circle. The referee drops the puck. Both players try to get the puck. They try to pass to their teammates. Each team then tries to get the puck in the other team's net.

**Fast Fact!**
**Face-offs** are used to start play again if the game has been stopped by the referee.

# Periods

A hockey game has three **periods**. Players leave the ice between periods. They take a break.

Skating makes the ice rough. At some rinks, a special machine cleans the ice between periods. When the ice is smooth, the teams return to the ice.

# Penalty Box

There are lots of rules in hockey. You can't trip other players. You can't hook others with your stick. You must play fair!

If a player breaks a rule, the referee calls a penalty. The player might have to go to the **penalty box**. He must stay in the box for a few minutes.

**Fast Fact!**
In adult hockey, players **check**, or push each other.
In kids' hockey, checking is against the rules.

**17**

A team can't replace a player in the penalty box. Now the other team has one more player on the ice! They have a good chance to score.

**Fast Fact!**
When a team has an extra player, it is called a power play.

The teams pass the puck. They make quick turns and fast stops. They work together to send the puck to the net. When they get the puck past the goal line, they score!

At the final whistle, the team with the most goals wins.

**Fast Fact!**
A team scores only when the puck crosses the red goal line.

# Glossary

**check** (CHEK): To check is to push another player.

**face-off** (FACE-off): A way to start or restart a game. Two players face each other and the referee drops the puck between them.

**face-off circle** (FACE-off SIR-cul): One of five circles around some face-off spots. Only the referee and the two players in the face-off are allowed in the circle.

**face-off spots** (FACE-off SPOTS): Dots on the ice where a face-off can happen. There are nine face-off spots on the rink.

**goalie** (GOHL-ee): A hockey player who stays near the goal and stops the puck from going into the net is called a goalie.

**pads** (PADS): Gear that protects the body. Pads can be built into hockey clothes (like ice hockey pants) or put on separately (like shin guards).

**penalty box** (PEN-uhl-tee BOX): A spot off the ice where players sit if they have broken the rules is called the penalty box.

**periods** (PEER-ee-udz): Set amounts of time that the players stay on the ice. Hockey games have three periods, usually twenty minutes each.

**puck** (PUK): The rubber disk that ice hockey players hit across the ice. It is about the size of a can of tuna.

**zones** (ZONES): The three areas in an ice hockey rink separated by blue lines. The three zones are the defensive zone (the area near the team's net), the offensive zone (the area near the opponent's net), and the neutral zone (the middle of the ice).

# To Learn More

### In the Library

Robinson, Tom. *Hockey: Math at the Rink*.
Mankato, MN: The Child's World, 2013.

Savage, Jeff. *Super Hockey Infographics*.
Minneapolis, MN: Lerner Publications, 2015.

Sports Illustrated for Kids. *Face-Off! Top
10 Lists of Everything in Hockey*. New
York, NY: Time Inc. Books, 2015.

### On the Web

Visit our Web site for links about hockey:
**childsworld.com/links**

Note to Parents, Teachers, and Librarians: We routinely verify
our Web links to make sure they are safe and active sites.
So encourage your readers to check them out!

# Index

## About the Author

Kara L. Laughlin is an artist and writer who lives in Virginia with her husband, three kids, two guinea pigs, and a dog. She is the author of two dozen nonfiction books for kids.